Windsor Castle

England's Royal Fortress

By Jacqueline A. Ball

Consultant: Stephen F. Brown, Director
Institute of Medieval Philosophy and Theology, Boston College

BEARPORT
PUBLISHING COMPANY, INC.

New York, New York

Credits

Cover, title page, Photodisc / Fotosearch.

Background portrait throughout, Getty images; 4-5, Pawel Libera / CORBIS; 6, 8, British Library Images Online; 9, Dallas & John Heaton / Alamy; 10, The Royal Collection © 2004, Her Majesty Queen Elizabeth II; 11, Getty Images; 12, Indexstock; 12-13, Adam Woolfitt / CORBIS; 14-15, 16-17, Mary Evans Picture Library; 17, Mary Evans, Douglas McCarthy / Mary Evans Picture Library; 18, Gianni Dagli Orti / CORBIS; 18-19, A Staircase, Windsor Castle, from 'Royal Residences', engraved by W. J. Bennett, pub. by William Henry Pyne (1769-1843), 1818 (aquatint), Wild, Charles (1781-1835) (after) / Private Collection, The Stapleton Collection / www.bridgeman.co.uk; 20-21, Gary Trotter; Eye Ubiquitous / CORBIS; 21 top, Tim Graham / CORBIS; 21 (bottom), Tim Graham / CORBIS; 22-23, AP Photo / Richard Lewis; 24 (top), Frank B. Blackburn / Worldwide Picture Library / Alamy; 24 (bottom), Jonathan Leigh / Science Photo Library / Photo Researchers, Inc.; 24-25, David Ford; 26-27, Rodica Prato; 27, Ivan J. Belcher / Worldwide Picture Library / Alamy; 29, Stan Kujawa / Alamy.

Design and production by Dawn Beard Creative, Triesta Hall of Blu-Design, and Octavo Design and Production, Inc.

Library of Congress Cataloging-in-Publication Data

Ball, Jacqueline A.
  Windsor Castle: England's royal fortress / by Jacqueline A. Ball; consultant, Stephen Brown.
    p. cm. — (Castles, palaces & tombs)
  Includes bibliographical references and index.
  ISBN 1-59716-005-9 (lib. bdg.)—ISBN 1-59716-028-8 (pbk.)
  1. Windsor Castle—History—Juvenile literature. I. Brown, Stephen F. II. Title. III. Series.

DA690.W76B35 2005
942.2'96—dc22

2004020993

For more information, write to Bearport Publishing Company, Inc., 101 Fifth Avenue, Suite 6R, New York, New York 10003. Printed in the United States of America.

1 2 3 4 5 6 7 8 9 10

Table of Contents

Lady in Black

The year was 1897. Carr Glynn, a castle guard, sat reading alone in the quiet library of Windsor Castle. At least, he thought he was alone. Suddenly, he heard a noise. Then a woman dressed in black walked by him.

Windsor Castle

Glynn followed the woman. Soon, however, she disappeared. The guard was puzzled. The woman looked like a painting he had seen of Queen Elizabeth the First. There was only one problem. Elizabeth had died 300 years before. The guard had just seen her ghost!

Windsor Castle has been called the most haunted castle in England.

Hated and Feared

Long before Queen Elizabeth, a **ruler** named William the Conqueror built Windsor Castle. William was **duke** of a part of France called Normandy.

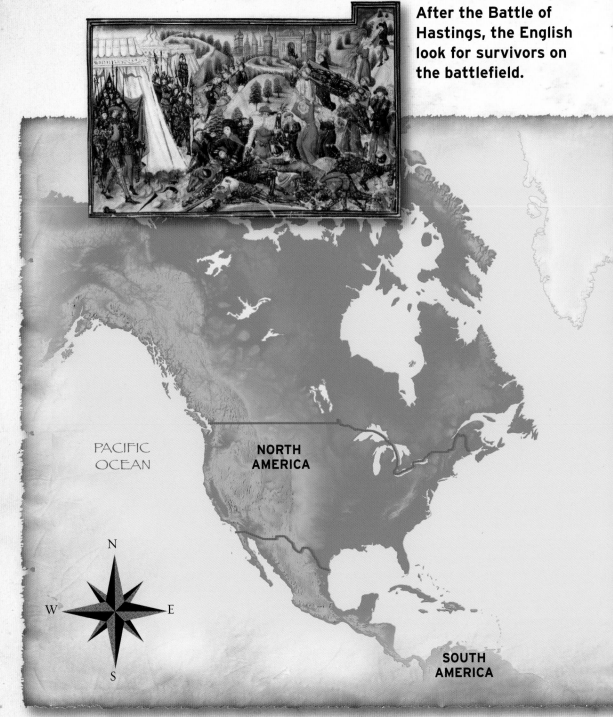

After the Battle of Hastings, the English look for survivors on the battlefield.

PACIFIC OCEAN

NORTH AMERICA

N

W   E

S

SOUTH AMERICA

William wanted much more power than he had in Normandy. So, in 1066, his army attacked England. They won a famous battle at a place called Hastings. William then became the king of England. He decided to live in London.

William did cruel things to show his new power. He took people's land and burned their crops. People hated and feared him.

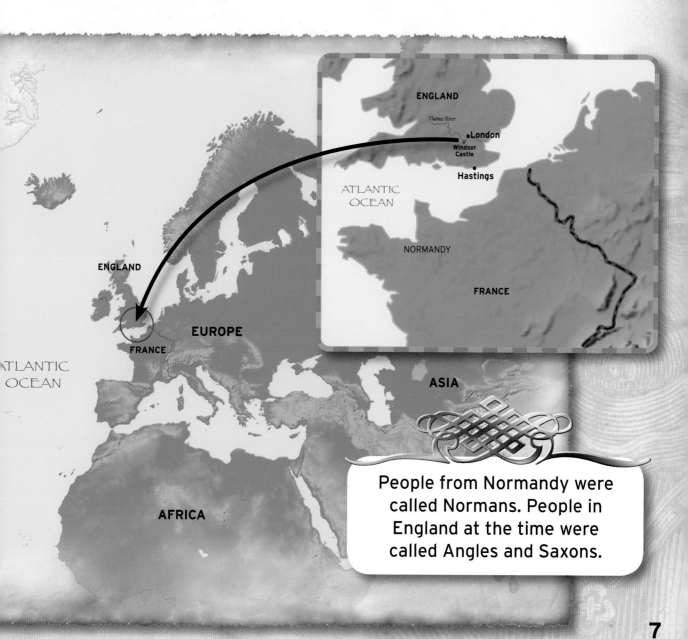

People from Normandy were called Normans. People in England at the time were called Angles and Saxons.

7

Enemies Everywhere

Even as a boy, William knew he had enemies. When he became a duke at age seven, people tried to **kidnap** him. These people wanted to take over Normandy. William was moved from place to place so kidnappers couldn't find him. Sometimes he was pulled out of bed in the middle of the night to run and hide.

William, Duke of Normandy, lands with his army in England.

By the time he became king, William knew how to protect himself. He built a ring of nine castles around London, the capital of England. Now his men could fight off attackers coming from any direction.

William's father was the first Duke of Normandy. William got the title when his father died in a battle.

The Tower of London was one of William's castles. Today, it holds the Crown Jewels.

Safe at Windsor

Windsor Castle was part of William's ring of castles. It was built out of wood. It stood on a cliff above the Thames River in the town of Windsor. From its tower, guards could open fire on attackers coming by land or by water. They could stop enemy ships heading down the river to London.

Windsor Castle during William's time

The tower was on a mound of earth. A big ditch called a **moat** was dug around it. A high fence was inside the moat. The fence and moat helped keep enemies away from William.

WILLIAM THE CONQUEROR.

This kind of castle building was called *motte and bailey. Motte* means "mound." *Bailey* was the yard where the tower and other buildings sat.

11

Improving the Castle

William's ring of castles protected him well. He ruled for 21 years, until he died in an accident. Later kings made **improvements** at Windsor Castle.

In about 1173, King Henry the Second added a high stone wall with buildings inside called a shell keep. Stone was stronger than wood. It also wouldn't burn.

A coat of arms at Windsor Castle

King Henry also built a stone tower inside the keep. It was called the Round Tower. Later rulers made the Round Tower even taller. They also added **cannons** inside.

Today the Round Tower is about 100 feet high. It can be seen from many miles away.

A Prison and a Chapel

In the 1300s, King Edward the Third used the castle as a prison. Back then, someone could be put to death for stealing a deer from Windsor Forest. The bodies were hung from Curfew Tower. They were a warning to others.

Inside Curfew Tower, illustrated by George M. Henton, 1908

King Edward captured the kings of Scotland and France during wars. He held them at Windsor Castle until their governments paid a **ransom**. Then he used the money to repair and rebuild the castle.

King Edward added a church. It was called St. George's **Chapel**. He built it for his special group of **knights**, the Order of the Garter.

Edward, Prince of Wales was the oldest son of King Edward the Third

King Edward's Order of the Garter was modeled after King Arthur's Knights of the Round Table.

A Strange Snowstorm

Inside St. George's Chapel are the **tombs** of ten English rulers. King Charles the First is buried there.

In 1648, Charles was forced from the throne. He was **accused** of being a criminal and kept prisoner at Windsor Castle. He was put to death the following year.

This part of the chapel holds the tombs of English royalty.

The day of King Charles' funeral had started bright and clear. As guards carried his **coffin** into the chapel, however, a snowstorm hit. White snowflakes piled up on the coffin. Many people thought the clean, white snow was a sign from the heavens. To them, it meant Charles was not a criminal.

King Charles the First

For over 600 years there has been a group of singers at St. George's Chapel. They sing during daily services.

Ghosts in the Castle

Some say the monarchs buried in St. George's Chapel don't lie still. King Henry the Eighth died in 1547. People say they've seen his ghost and heard it groaning.

How many ghosts have passed through the great hallways of Windsor Castle?

King Henry the Eighth in 1540

The queen's main **residence** is Buckingham Palace in London.

In the 1700s, King George the Third ruled at Windsor Castle. He became ill with a disease that made him act crazy. He acted so strangely that he was kept locked up. People say they've seen his ghost staring from the window of his room.

Windsor Castle has plenty of space for ghosts and living people. Today's ruler of England, Queen Elizabeth the Second, spends time there with her family.

Fire!

None of Windsor's ghosts has harmed the castle. However, Windsor Castle faced real danger on November 20, 1992. A hot light made a curtain catch on fire. The blaze roared for 15 hours. No one was hurt, but the fire damaged or destroyed about 100 rooms.

Fire at Windsor Castle

It took five years to **restore** the castle. Workers repaired floors, walls, and ceilings. They cleaned **soot** from paintings and fixed broken statues. The huge kitchen was rebuilt.

Outside, gardeners planted beautiful white roses and bushes. The castle was ready in time for the Queen's 50th wedding anniversary in 1997.

Restoring the castle

It took 1,500 workers to restore Windsor Castle.

William's Well

Windsor Castle looks about the same today as it did before the fire. It's once more used for ceremonies, balls, and weddings. Beautiful paintings by famous artists once again hang on the walls.

The Order of the Garter procession makes its way to St. George's Chapel in 2002.

Right after the fire, an amazing thing happened. Workers were clearing away a damaged part of the castle. There, they made a discovery. They found a well hidden in the ground. **Historians** decided it must have been the one used by William the Conqueror, over 900 years ago, in the first Windsor Castle.

When the queen is at the castle, a flag called the Royal Standard flies. If she is not there, only the British flag flies.

Visiting Windsor Castle

To visit the castle, you can take a train or bus from London to the town of Windsor. The castle stands high above the busy town.

Visitors like to walk through Windsor Great Park. It's part of the forest where royal men once hunted. They might pass Cranbourne Tower. King George the Fourth locked up his daughter here because she wouldn't marry the man he chose for her.

Windsor Great Park, fall

Windsor Great Park, spring

Park visitors walk past very old oak trees. Here, the sharpest eyes might spot Herne the Hunter. Herne was a deer hunter. People say he now haunts the park—wearing antlers.

Workers doing underground repair work found nests of poisonous spiders under Windsor Great Park in 2001.

Cranbourne Tower

The Changing of the Guard

At the castle, visitors can watch the Changing of the Guard at 11:00 a.m. almost every day. One group of guards goes off watch and another group arrives. Both groups march in colorful uniforms while a band plays.

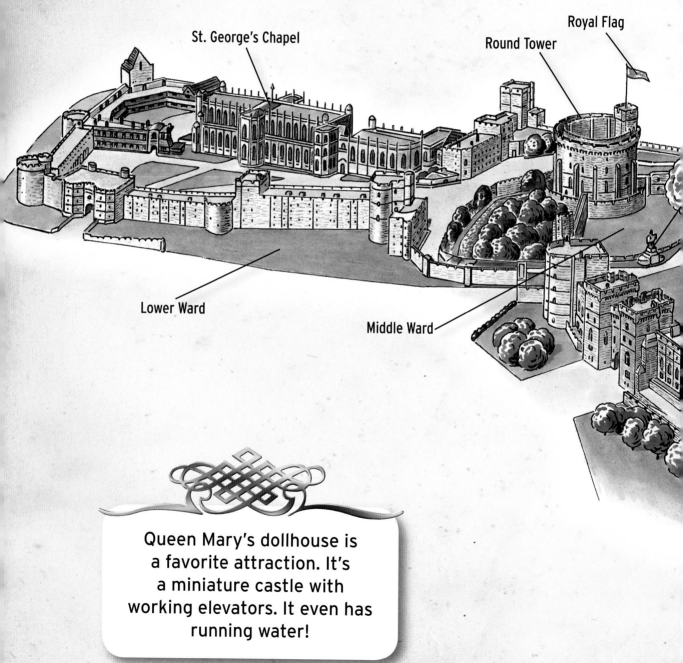

St. George's Chapel

Royal Flag

Round Tower

Lower Ward

Middle Ward

Queen Mary's dollhouse is a favorite attraction. It's a miniature castle with working elevators. It even has running water!

Inside, you can see beautiful rooms full of old treasures. Suits of **armor** and gold dinner plates are on display. It's no surprise that Windsor Castle was voted one of England's Seven Wonders.

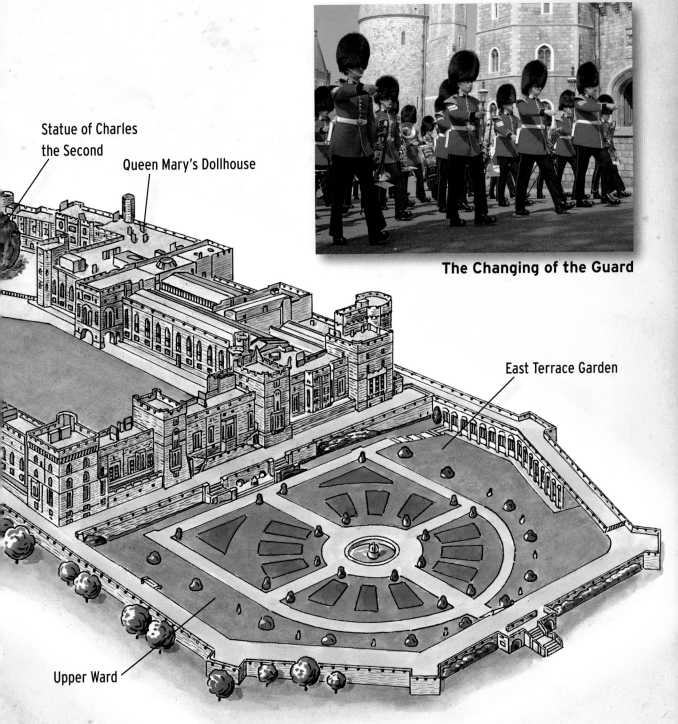

The Changing of the Guard

Statue of Charles the Second

Queen Mary's Dollhouse

East Terrace Garden

Upper Ward

Just the Facts

❧ The first castle William the Conqueror built was the Tower of London. It's now London's number one tourist attraction.

❧ Windsor Castle is divided into wards, or areas. Each ward is protected by its own walls and towers. These areas made the castle easier to guard.

❧ The Order of the Garter still meets at St. George's Chapel every year on St. George's Day, April 23.

❧ Queen Elizabeth the Second's grandfather was King George the Fifth. During World War I, he changed his family's last name to Windsor.

❧ Queen Elizabeth the Second has several homes besides Buckingham Palace and Windsor Castle. They are:

  Kensington and St. James palaces in London

  Balmoral Castle and the Palace of Holyroodhouse in Scotland

  Sandringham House in Norfolk

Timeline

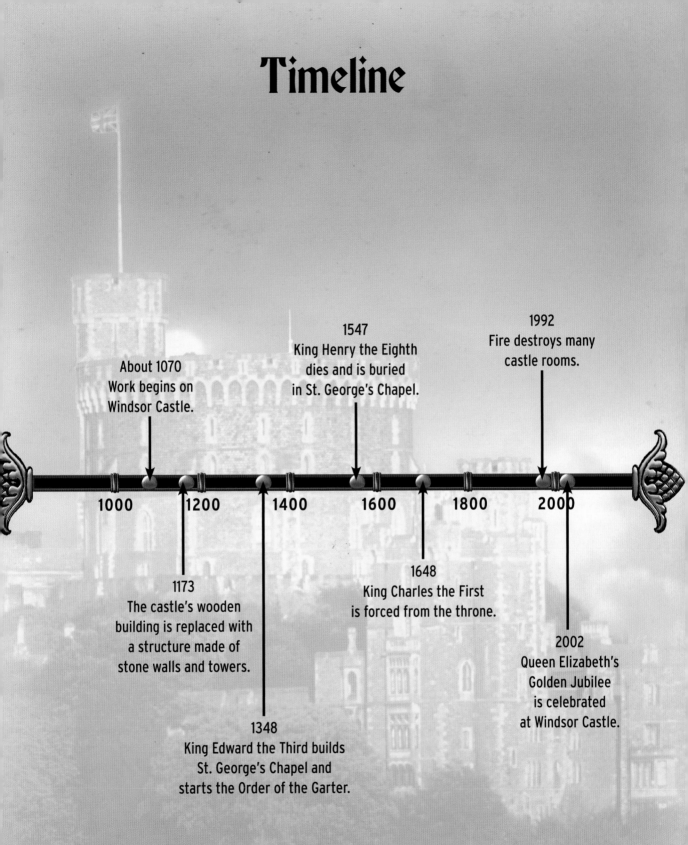

About 1070
Work begins on
Windsor Castle.

1547
King Henry the Eighth
dies and is buried
in St. George's Chapel.

1992
Fire destroys many
castle rooms.

1000   1200   1400   1600   1800   2000

1173
The castle's wooden
building is replaced with
a structure made of
stone walls and towers.

1648
King Charles the First
is forced from the throne.

2002
Queen Elizabeth's
Golden Jubilee
is celebrated
at Windsor Castle.

1348
King Edward the Third builds
St. George's Chapel and
starts the Order of the Garter.

Glossary

accused (uh-KYOOZD) blamed for or charged with a crime or doing something wrong

armor (AR-mur) a suit of metal worn to protect the body in battle

cannons (KAN-uhnz) large guns set on a base that fire large metal balls

chapel (CHAP-uhl) a small church

coffin (KAWF-in) a long box in which a dead person is buried

duke (DOOK) in England, a person who holds the rank just below a prince

historians (hiss-TOR-ee-uhnz) people who study events and people of the past

improvements (im-PROOV-muhntz) things done to make something better

kidnap (KID-*nap*) to take someone by force and keep the person as a prisoner in order to get money

knights (NITES) soldiers who fought on horseback during the Middle Ages (a period in Europe from about the years 500 to 1450)

moat (MOHT) a deep, wide ditch dug around a castle and filled with water for protection against enemies

ransom (RAN-suhm) money demanded in return for setting a kidnapped, or captive, person free

residence (REZ-uh-duhnss) a house or place where someone lives

restore (ri-STOR) to bring something back to its original condition

ruler (ROO-lur) someone who rules, or has power over, a country

soot (SUT) a fine black powder that is made when something is burned

tombs (TOOMZ) graves, rooms, or buildings in which dead bodies are buried

Bibliography

Forman, Joan. *Haunted Royal Homes.* Norwich, UK: Jarrold Publishing (1987).

Howard, Philip. *The Royal Palaces.* Boston, MA: Gambit Incorporated (1970).

Howarth, David. *1066: The Year of the Conquest.* New York, NY: Barnes & Noble Books (1977).

Jones, Richard. *Haunted Castles of Britain and Ireland.* New York, NY: Barnes and Noble Books (2003).

Read More

Boraas, Tracey. *England.* Mankato, MN: Capstone Press (2003).

Dargie, Richard. *Knights and Castles.* Chicago, IL: Raintree (1998).

Farman, John. *The Short and Bloody History of Knights.* Minneapolis, MN: Lerner Publications (2003).

Frost, Helen. *Castles: Towers, Dungeons, Moats, and More.* Mankato, MN: Capstone Press (2003).

Learn More Online

Visit these Web sites to learn more about Windsor Castle:

www.berkshirehistory.com/castles/windsor_cast.html

www.berkshirehistory.com/kids

www.royal.gov.uk/output/Page1.asp

www.windsor.gov.uk/attractions/castle.htm

Index

About the Author

Jacqueline A. Ball has written and produced
more than one hundred books for kids and adults.
She lives in New York City and Old Lyme, Connecticut.